COLOR CABLES

Color Cables

ISBN 13 (print): 978-1-937513-86-3
First edition

Published by Cooperative Press
http://www.cooperativepress.com

Patterns, text and charts ©2018 Andi Smith
Photos ©2018 Jenn Kidd
Models: Jennifer Davis, Breaya Wilson, Grace Kontur, Danielle Marx, Daniella Cortez

If you have questions or comments about this book, or need information about licensing, custom editions, special sales, or academic/corporate purchases, please contact Cooperative Press: info@cooperativepress.com or 10252 Berea Rd, Cleveland, Ohio 44102 USA

For Cooperative Press

Senior Editor: Shannon Okey
Technical Editor: Meg Roke

COLOR CABLES

COOPERATIVE PRESS
Cleveland, Ohio

PATTERNS

INTRO

I adore working cables, and for many years I've enjoyed working color cables: adding a second color to the cable field to truly make those cable stitches pop. In this book, I show you not only how to work with two colors but also with a multitude of colors to make your cables outstanding!

The first half of the book gives you the fundamentals, as well as tips and tricks you will need to successfully work color cables, including written and visual tutorials, and step by step small practice swatches to truly master each technique. The second half of the book includes patterns that I designed to showcase your growing skills, taking you from beginner to color cable mastery.

NEED TO KNOW

Let's talk color cable basics, everything from choosing the right yarns to the most effective ways to manipulate them for the best results.

Note: throughout the book, wherever you see a link to a website, it will be clickable in the digital edition!

YARN CHOICE

There are two main rules I try to follow when working with color cables:

First, the same yarn weight and fiber content really go a long way towards creating a luscious knitted fabric. I prefer to work with wool/silk blends, but these projects have made even the most lowly of big box yarns look scrumptious!

I'll be honest and admit that I break this first rule frequently, indeed one of the patterns, Blackstar (page 93), is worked with a DK yarn for the cables and fingering weight for the background purls. It took quite a bit of math and stitch wrangling to make the different yarn gauges work, so when you're first starting out, aim for same weight yarns until you've mastered the ability to make uniform stitches using the techniques provided.

My second rule focuses on color. If you're like me, you'll be looking at patterns, raiding your stash, pairing up hanks and skeins, and deciding what goes with what. Learn from my many mistakes, and never EVER pair two similar colors together, whether they're slightly different hues, or a solid and variegated that have the same color in them.

Even an inch or two of the same color in a variegated yarn creates a knitted field of mud. All your hard work will go down the drain. High contrast pairings really do work the best. Take your choices out into the sunlight and really inspect those variegated skeins for similar colors.

HOW TO HOLD YOUR YARN

There are several ways to hold strands of yarn for colorwork — holding both strands in the right hand, both in the left, or one strand in each hand. I prefer to hold both strands of yarn in my right hand. Fortunately, the techniques I describe work equally well for of the methods listed above. Whatever way you are comfortable holding two yarns will be perfect for these techniques.

FLOATS

One thing to keep in mind is that your floats need to be carried across the wrong side of your work. If you're working flat rows, that means that for right side rows (RS), your floats will be facing away from you, and when you're working wrong side rows (WS), your floats will be facing you.

If you've worked with two or more colors in a row of knitting before, then you know the importance of float tension. Too tight, and you end up with a very dense fabric that is unusable; too loose, and your result is a floppy hole-y mush.

To make your floats lay smoothly across your stitches, work them as follows:

- Knit or purl as many stitches as the pattern indicates.
- Before changing colors, make sure both yarns are at the back of your work.
- Arrange the stitches on the right hand needle (RH) across the needle in a good approximation of your gauge.
- Bring the new color yarn across the back of these stitches and work the next stitch allowing a small bit of ease in your float. You may have to re-adjust the float after your first stitch, but within a few rows of work, it will become second nature.

Use this methodology whether you're carrying yarn across two stitches or twenty-two. As long as your RH needle stitches are spread out to gauge, and your float is laying loosely across them, then your knitted fabric will be successful. I've found that there is no need to anchor your floats. In my previous color cable collection, the pattern French Quarter had a 17-st float. I've knitted and worn two of them, and never had a problem with floats catching and pulling. Be brave! Let those floats nestle amongst your stitches without anchoring them down.

Floats across wrong side of work

AN EASY TIP TO AVOID HOLES

When you're working flat, as your colors meet for the first time on each row, wrap one yarn around the other to avoid holes. If you wrap clockwise on RS rows, and counter-clockwise on WS rows, then your yarns will not twist.

MC is blue yarn, CC is terracotta yarn

Place MC over the top, and to the left of the CC yarn.

Bring CC up over MC, and to the right, ready to work next st.

HOW THE PATTERNS WORK

Each of the patterns in *Color Cables* offer both written instructions and charts. It's helpful in the beginning to grab a couple of colored pencils and spend a little time with your pattern. For charts, color your purl stitches one color, and your cables/knits another.

For written instructions, color all main color (MC) instructions one color, and all contrasting color (CC) instructions another. This gives you a clear visualization of the flow of the stitches, which can be helpful when first learning.

SUBSTITUTING YARNS

The majority of patterns in *Color Cables* are worked in fingering weight yarn; however, there's nothing stopping you from working them in a different weight. As long as you use two yarns that are the same weight and fiber content, then you're good to go. Obviously, yardage and measurements will be different, but a little experimentation will garner great results.

DON'T PANIC

Two or three rounds in, you'll notice that the purl columns stick out more than the knit ones. Don't panic! After a few more rows or rounds, the purls sink into the background and the knit stitches bounce right back to the front.

HOW TO AVOID LADDERS

When you're working in the round, and are at the start of a new round, give those first and second stitches a little tug after knitting them. It helps to avoid ladders in your work, and evens out the gauge. Similarly, with color cables, it helps to do that at each color change in your work. Whilst this seems laborious at first, it soon becomes an un-noticed part of your knitting process and really helps to make your stitches even and your overall work look spectacular.

INTARSIA CABLES

Once you master working with two different colors, your options become truly unlimited. The popularity of mini-skein kits truly lends itself to color cables. Using each skein for a column of cables gives a truly stunning result.

Work as you would any intarsia or colorwork project by wrapping two colors the first time they meet on any row to avoid holes.

There are lots of ways to keep your mini-skeins organized, experiment to see what works best for you. I prefer to use mini balls about 15 yards long. There are more ends to weave in, but if they get in a tangle, they're easier to reorganize than a whole skein.

Mesh makeup brush protectors (https://amzn.to/2CNGzY3) are a cheap yet handy way to stop them from unwinding as you work. See the photo below for miniature balls in use.

WET BLOCKING

As you bind off your project, it will look amazing, finished, and ready to wear. However, take the time to wet block your completed project. This is crucial to finishing your project and gives it a polished, professional look. Most importantly, it helps settle the stitches into their places, evens out the floats, and just helps your yarn to bloom. I recommend wet blocking for all *Color Cable* projects as described below:

* Immerse your project in luke warm water with a small amount of wool wash added. Make sure it is completely submerged, and leave it for at least a couple of hours.
* Gently squeeze out the water.
* Wrap your knitting in a towel, and squeeze out more water.
* Gently shape your project to measurements and allow to completely dry. Pin into place, if necessary.

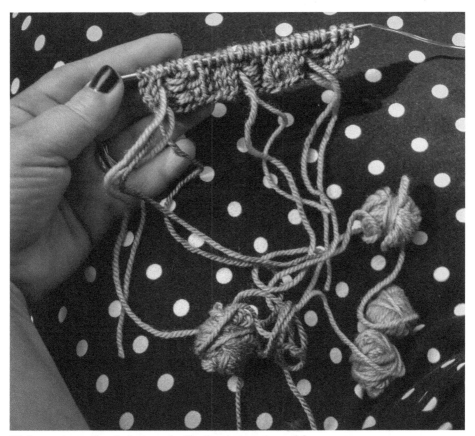

Using 15-yard miniature balls for intarsia cables.

STARTER SWATCHES

If you are new to color cables, the following small practice swatches will provide a perfect step-by-step introduction to techniques used throughout the book. Starting with using two colors, followed by the various cable stitches used, and ending with the Knot Stitch (which is deliciously fiddly and fun to knit), you'll be an expert in no time!

If you prefer to work from a chart, it's worth taking a couple of minutes now to color in your chart, with all the purl stitches one color, and your knit stitches another. This gives a great visual representation of how your cables will flow, and an idea of what your final swatch will look like.

If you'd rather work from the written instructions, grab two colored pencils, and color as follows:

- For instructions in the round, color all knit sts in CC, and all purl sts in MC, unless instructed otherwise.
- For instructions worked flat, on RS rows, color all purls in MC color, and all knits in CC color; for WS rows, color all knits in MC and all purls in CC, unless otherwise specified.

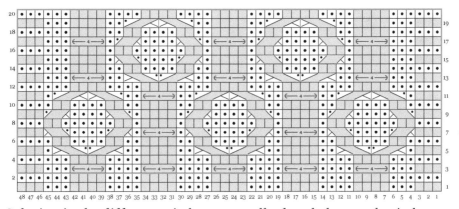

Coloring in the different stitch types really does help your brain keep track of what you're doing as you knit.

HOW TO READ CHARTS

If you're working flat:

- Right side rows are read from right to left. Purls are worked in MC and knits are worked in CC. Cables and special stitches are worked as directed in specific instructions for that pattern.
- Wrong side rows are read from left to right. Purls are worked in CC and knits are worked in MC.

If you're working in the round:

- Each round is read from right to left. All purls are worked in MC and all knits are worked in CC unless otherwise specified.

HOW TO READ WRITTEN INSTRUCTIONS

In this chapter, written instructions are given with either an MC or CC before them. In the rest of the book, instructions do not have this prefix.

If you're working flat:

- On right side rows, purls are worked in MC and knits are worked in CC.
- On wrong side rows, purls are worked in CC and knits in MC. Cables and special stitches are worked as directed in specific instructions for that pattern.

If you're working in the round:

- All purls are in MC and all knits are in CC unless otherwise specified.

WORK AS THEY APPEAR

"Work as they appear" is a sentence often used in knitting patterns. This means to knit the knit stitches and purl the purl stitches. If a stitch is worked in MC, then continue to work it in MC. If a stitch is worked in CC, then continue to work it in CC, unless otherwise specified.

The MC symbol

| mc |

One of the most pleasing aspects of working color cables is the seamless field of reverse stockinette behind the cables. I've found that in order to maintain that seamless field, sometimes a purl stitch had to be knitted to avoid differently colored purl bumps. If you're like me, that one tiny purl bump will be the only thing you can see in the whole finished piece. It will stand out like a glaring beacon! To avoid this, wherever you see this symbol in a chart, work that stitch as directed. Written instructions will let you know specifically what color to use for that stitch.

THREE STITCH WRAP SWATCH

Top Row: MC Blue, CC Terracotta, front and back
Bottom Row: MC Terracotta, CC Blue, front and back

Patterns that use this technique
- Lady Stardust mitts page 45
- White Light / White Heat scarf page 53

What you'll learn:
This pattern is a great introduction to working with two colors of yarn at the same time. You'll learn the best way to hold both yarns, and practice your single stitch float length, as well as learning how to work a three-stitch wrap. The soothing motion of knitting with one color, and purling with another will soon become second nature with this simple pattern. Whether you are a thrower or a picker, you'll quickly figure out the best way to hold your yarns, and the motions will become automatic after just a few rows.

Stitches Used
Long-tail cast on or Italian Two Color cast on: http://bit.ly/italian2color
Knit
Purl
Wrap st

Techniques
For a RS row: [With MC, p1, place MC yarn to back of work, with CC, k1, bring MC yarn to front] 8 times, with MC, p1.

For a WS row: [With MC, k1, bring MC yarn to WS of work (the side facing you), with CC, p1, bring MC yarn to RS of work (the side NOT facing you)] 8 times, with MC, k1.

Wrap stitch
• [Slip next 3 sts to RH needle, bring CC yarn to front, slip 3 sts from RH needle to LH needle, bring CC yarn loosely across 3 sts and place in back] 3 times, CC k1, MC p1, CC k1.

Pattern Notes
On the RS of your work, purl stitches are worked in MC, and knit stitches are worked in CC.

On the WS of your work, knit stitches are worked in MC, and purl stitches are worked in CC.

The Swatch
You have two options for your cast on for this swatch. If you're new to working with two colors of yarn at the same time, cast on 17 sts using your MC yarn. If you're feeling adventurous, cast on 17 sts using Italian Two Color cast on, using MC as the first yarn, and CC as the second.

Row 1 (RS): [MC p1, CC k1] 8 times, MC p1.
Row 2 (WS): [MC k1, CC p1] 8 times, MC k1.
Rows 3, 5 and 7: Repeat Row 1.
Rows 4, 6 and 8: Repeat Row 2.
Row 9: [MC p1, 3 st wrap] four times, MC p1.
Row 10: Repeat Row 2.
Row 11: Repeat Row 1.
Row 12: Repeat Row 2.
Row 13: MC P1, CC k1, [MC p1, 3 st wrap] three times, MC p1, CC k1, MC p1.
Row 14: Repeat Row 2.
Row 15: Repeat Row 1.
Row 16: Repeat Row 2.
Row 17: Repeat Row 9.
Rows 18, 20 and 22: Repeat Row 2.
Rows 19 and 21: As Row 1.
Bind off in pattern.
Wet block. (blocking instructions page 13)

Analyze your swatch. Does everything lay smoothly, or is your fabric puckered, or loose?

- If it's puckered, that means your floats are too tight. Work another swatch and either go up a needle size, or consciously work on allowing the floats to sit more loosely. If it's very tight you may need to do both.
- If your fabric is loose and floppy, try going down a needle size, or pulling your floats slightly—ever so slightly—tighter.

▢ RS: Knit WS: Purl

▣ RS: Purl WS: Knit

←— 3 —→ 3 st wrap

THREE STITCH WRAP SWATCH CHART

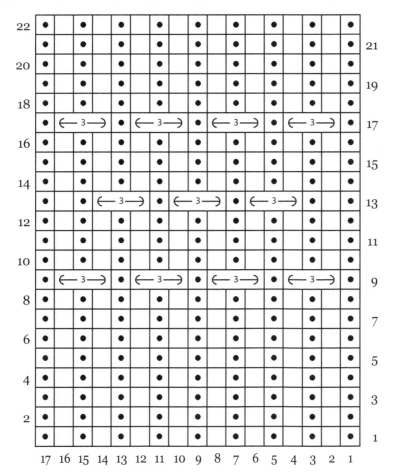

THREE STITCH WRAP TUTORIAL

With yarn in back, slip 3 sts to from right hand needle to left.

Bring yarn to front of work, slip 3 sts back to left hand needle.

Repeat these two steps three times.

With CC, k1.

With MC, p1, with CC, k1.

2/1 LPC 2/1 RPC SWATCH

swatch front (unblocked)

swatch back (unblocked)

Patterns that use this technique
- Soul Love scarf page 87
- Moonage Daydream hat page 81
- Oh! You Pretty Things shawl page 75
- Fascination cowl page 59
- Up The Hill Backwards scarf page 67
- White Light / White Heat Scarf page 53

What you'll learn:
How to cable using two colors
Working floats over 2, 3, and 4 sts

Stitches Used
long tail cast on
knit
purl
2/1 LpC
2/1 RpC

Techniques
- 2/1 LpC (2/1 Left purl Cross) — slip 2 sts to cn, hold in front of work, MC p1, CC k 2 sts from cable needle
- 2/1 RpC (2/1 Right purl Cross) — slip 1 st to cn, hold in back of work, CC k2, MC p1 from cable needle

Pattern Notes
On the RS of your work, purl stitches are worked in MC, and knit stitches are worked in CC. On the WS of your work, knit stitches are worked in MC, and purl stitches are worked in CC.

The Swatch

Using MC, and the Long-tail method, cast on 18 sts.
Row 1: MC p2, [CC k2, MC p2] four times.
Row 2: MC k2, [CC p2, MC k2] four times.
Row 3. [MC p2, 2/1 LpC, 2/1 RpC] twice, MC p2.
Row 4 (and all even rows): Work sts as they appear.
Row 5: MC p3, 2/2 RC, MC p4, 2/2 LC, p3.
Row 7: MC p2, [2/1 RpC, 2/1 LpC, MC p2] twice.
Row 9: MC p2, CC k2, MC p2, 2/1 LpC, 2/1 RpC, MC p2, CC k2, MC p2.
Row 11: MC p2, CC k2, MC p3, 2/2 RC, MC p3, CC k2, MC p2.
Row 13: MC p2, CC k2, MC p2, 2/1 RpC, 2/1 LpC, MC p2, CC k2, MC p2.
Row 14: Work sts as they appear. Break CC.
Using MC only, bind off in pattern.

Wet block. (blocking instructions page 13).

Analyze your swatch. Does everything lay smoothly, or is your fabric puckered, or loose?

- If it's puckered, that means your floats are too tight.Work another swatch and either go up a needle size, or consciously work on allowing the floats to sit more loosely. If it's very tight you may need to do both.
- If your fabric is loose and floppy, try going down a needle size, or pulling your floats slightly—ever so slightly—tighter.

2/1 LPC OR 2/1 RPC SWATCH CHART

☐	RS: Knit WS: Purl
☐•	RS: Purl WS: Knit
⟋⟍	2/1 LpC
⟋⟍	2/1 RpC
⟋⟍	2/2 LC
⟍⟋	2/2 RC

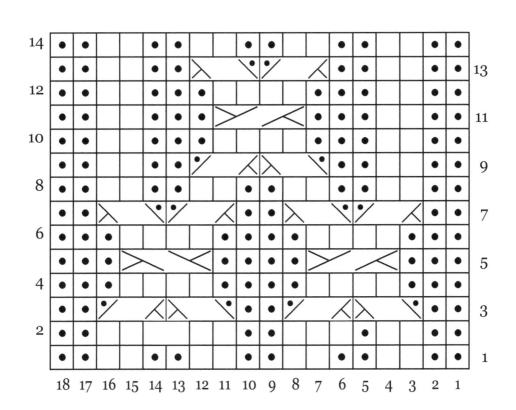

2/1 LPC TUTORIAL

Slip 2 sts to cn, hold in front of work.

MC p1, CC k2 from cable needle.

2/1 RPC TUToRiAL

Slip next st to cn, hold in back of work.

CC k2, MC p1 from cable needle.

2/2 LC, 2/2 RC, 2/2 LPC, 2/2 RPC SWATCH

swatch front (unblocked)

swatch back (unblocked)

Patterns that use this technique
- Blackstar cowl page 93
- Moonage Daydream hat page 81
- Soul Love scarf page 87
- Oh! You Pretty Things shawl page 75
- Fascination cowl page 59
- Up The Hill Backwards scarf page 67
- White Light / White Heat scarf page 53

What you'll learn
How to cable using two colors
How to work longer floats

Stitches Used
knit
purl
2/2 LC
2/2 RC
2/2 LpC
2/2 RpC

Techniques
- 2/2 LC (2/2 Left Cross) — slip 2 sts to cn, hold in front, CC k2, CC k2 from cn
- 2/2 RC (2/2 Right Cross) — slip 2 sts to cn, hold in back, CC k2, CC k2 from cn
- 2/2 LpC (2/2 Left purl Cross) — slip 2 sts to cn, hold in front, MC p2, CC k2 from cn
- 2/2 RpC (2/2 Right purl Cross) — slip 2 sts to cn, hold in back, CC k2, MC p2 from cn

Pattern Notes
On the RS of your work, purl stitches are worked in MC, and knit stitches are worked in CC. On the WS of your work, knit stitches are worked in MC, and purl stitches are worked in CC.

The Swatch

Using MC, and long-tail method, cast on 20 sts.
Rows 1 and 3 (RS): MC p2, CC k2, MC p4, CC k4, MC p4, CC k2, MC p2.
Rows 2 and 4 (WS): MC k2, CC p2, MC k4, CC p4, MC k4, CC p2, MC k2.
Row 5: MC p2, [2/2 LpC, 2/2 RpC] twice, MC p2.
Rows 6 and 8: [MC k4, CC p4] twice, MC k4.
Row 7: [MC p4, CC k4] twice, MC p4.
Row 9: MC p4, 2/2 RC, MC p4, 2/2 LC, MC p4.
Rows 10 and 12: As Row 6.
Row 11: As row 7.
Row 13: MC p2, [2/2 RpC, 2/2 LpC] twice, MC p2.
Rows 14 and 16: As Row 6.
Row 15: As Row 7.
Bind off in pattern.

Wet block. (blocking instructions page 13)

Analyze your swatch. Does everything lay smoothly, or is your fabric puckered, or loose?

- If it's puckered, that means your floats are too tight.Work another swatch and either go up a needle size, or consciously work on allowing the floats to sit more loosely. If it's very tight you may need to do both.
- If your fabric is loose and floppy, try going down a needle size, or pulling your floats slightly—ever so slightly—tighter.

2/2 LPC, 2/2 RPC, 2/2 LC, 2/2 RC SWATCH CHART

RS: Knit WS: Purl

RS: Purl WS: Knit

2/2 LpC

2/2 RpC

2/2 LC

2/2 RC

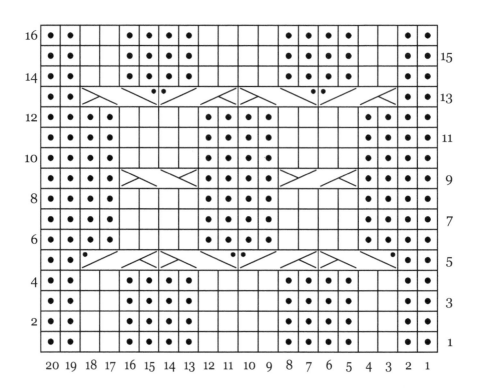

2/2 LC TUTORIAL

Sl 2 sts to cn, hold in front of work.

K2.

K2 from cn.

2/2 RC Tutorial

Sl2 to cn, hold in back of work.

K2.

K2 from cn.

2/2 LPC Tutorial

Sl2 to cn, hold in front of work.

With MC, p2.

With CC k2 from cn.

2/2 RPC TUTORIAL

Sl 2 sts to cn, hold in back of work.

With CC, k2.

With MC p2 from cn.

KNOT STITCH SWATCH

swatch front (unblocked)

swatch back (unblocked)

Patterns that use this technique
• Rebel Rebel skirt, page 101

What you'll learn
How to work knot stitch
Multi-step cabling
When to use MC for knit sts on RS rows

Stitches Used
knit
purl
knot st
mc

Techniques
Knot stitch — with CC only:
• slip 4 sts to cn, hold in front
• K2, bring yarn to front
• Put left 2 sts from cn onto LH needle
• Move cn to back of work
• [P2 from LH needle, slide 2 purled sts back to LH needle] twice, p2 from LH needle
• K2 from cn

Pattern Notes
On the RS of your work, purl stitches are worked in MC, and knit stitches are worked in CC — unless otherwise stated.

On the WS of your work, knit stitches are worked in MC, and purl stitches are worked in CC — unless otherwise stated.

On Row 4, you'll notice that you work 6 purls in CC, rather than the established pattern. This is to make the knot worked on the following row flow in just one color.

On Row 6, you'll notice that what will become two purled stitches on the following row, are knitted in MC. This is done to avoid CC purl bumps showing and spoiling the flow of your work.

The Swatch

Using MC, and long-tail method, cast on 30 sts.

Rows 1 and 3 (RS): [MC p2, CC k2, MC p2, CC k2, MC p2] three times.
Row 2: [MC k2, CC p2, MC k2, CC p2, MC k2] three times.
Row 4: [MC k2, CC p6, MC k2] three times.
Row 5: [MC p2, knot stitch, MC p2] three times.
Row 6: [MC k2, CC p2, MC p2, CC p2, MC k2] three times.
Rows 7, and 9: As Row 1.
Rows 8, and 10: As Row 2.
Bind off in pattern.

Analyze your swatch. Does everything lay smoothly, or is your fabric puckered, or loose?

- If it's puckered, that means your floats are too tight.Work another swatch and either go up a needle size, or consciously work on allowing the floats to sit more loosely. If it's very tight you may need to do both.
- If your fabric is loose and floppy, try going down a needle size, or pulling your floats slightly—ever so slightly—tighter.

Wet block. (blocking instructions page 13)

KNOT STITCH SWATCH CHART

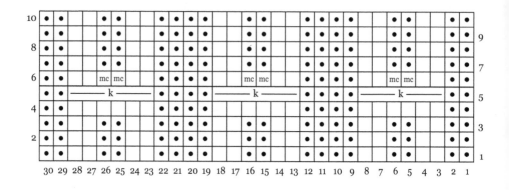

⬜ RS: Knit WS: Purl

mc WS: with MC, Purl

● RS: Purl WS: Knit

— k — Knot stitch

KNOT STITCH TUTORIAL

Rnd 5: MC p2, then working with CC only:

Slip next four sts to cn, hold in front of work.

K2.

Bring yarn to front of work, p2, slip 2 purled sts to LH needle.

Move cable needle to back of work.

[p2, slip two purled sts back to LH needle] twice.

Knit 2 sts from cn.

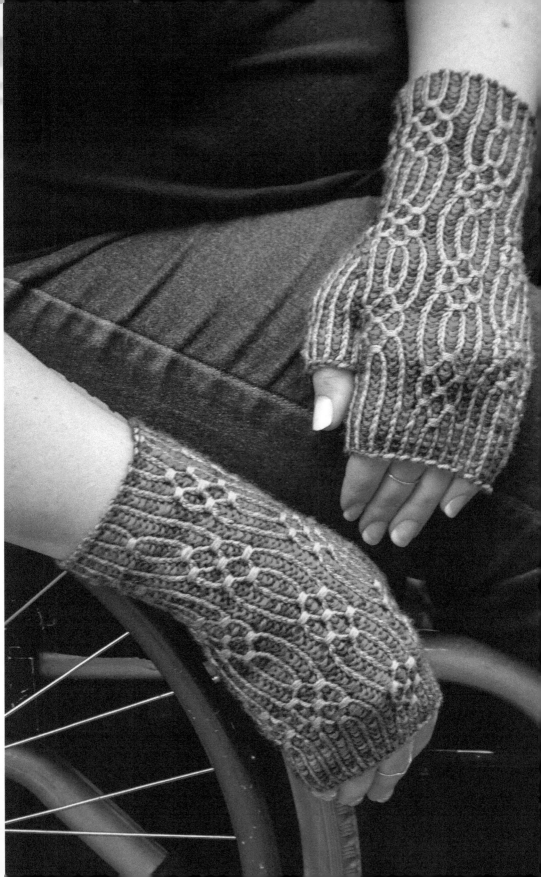

LADY STARDUST

This design is the perfect project for dipping your toes into the world of Color Cables. Not only do these fingerless mitts look more complex than they really are, but (and don't tell your friends this bit) they don't include cabling at all. The twisted rib and wrapped stitches give the illusion of cables without actually doing them! This project is also a prime example of how a brighter color can be used in the background with a softer color featured on the twisted rib and wrapped stitches.

REQUIRED SKILLS

Knitting in the round
Working wrap stitch from chart or written directions
Italian Two Color cast on

SIZE

Medium (Large)

FINISHED MEASUREMENTS

(to be worn with 0.5 inches / 1.25 cm negative ease)
9.75 inches / 24.75 cm tall x 7 (8) inches / 17.75 (20.25) cm circumference
Note: The mitts were the same measurements before and after blocking.

MATERIALS

Lorna's Laces Shepherd Sport (100% Superwash Merino; 200 yds / 183 m per 57 g / 2.01 oz skein), one skein in MC and CC
MC color: Sage: 1 skein or 100 (125) yds
CC color: Red Rover: 1 skein or 100 (125) yds
US#4 / 3.5 mm circular needles or four double-pointed needles, or size needed to obtain gauge
Stitch marker
Large-eyed, blunt needle

GAUGE

32 sts and 28 rnds = 4 inches / 10 cm in corrugated rib pattern, unblocked

PATTERN NOTES

Unless otherwise stated, all purl stitches are worked in MC and all knit stitches are worked in CC.

If working from the chart, it's helpful to color all the knit stitches in the color of your CC yarn, and the purl stitches the color of your MC yarn.

ABBREVIATIONS

CC- contrasting color
k - knit
k1tbl - knit 1 st through the back loop
LH - left hand
MC - main color
p - purl
patt - pattern
pm - place marker
RH - right hand
rnd(s) - round(s)
sm - slip marker
st(s) - stitch(es)
wyib - with CC yarn in back
wyif - with CC yarn in front

TECHNIQUES

- Italian Two Color Cast On — http://bit.ly/italian2color
- 3 st wrap — [wyib, slip 3 sts to RH needle, wyif, slip 3 sts back to LH needle] three times, CC k1, MC p1, CC k1 (see page 20 for 3 st wrap tutorial)
- M2pkp — make 2 purl. (CC p1, MC k1tbl, CC p1) into next purl st
- M1kp — make 1 knit. (MC ktbl, CC p1) into next st
- M1pk — make 1 purl. (CC p1, MC k1tbl) into next st
- M1pp — make 2 purl. (CC p1tbl, p1) into next st

PATTERN

Both mitts worked the same.
Using Italian Two color cast on method, cast on 48 (56) sts, starting with MC as the first color. Join to work in the round, adding a stitch marker to denote end of round.

Work 16 rnds of pattern, from either Lady Stardust chart, or written directions below.

Rnd 1 (and every odd rnd): *P1, k1tbl; repeat from * to end of rnd.
Rnd 2: *[P1, k1tbl] 1 (2) times, p1, 3 st wrap, [p1, k1tbl] twice, p1, 3 st wrap, [p1, k1tbl] twice, p1, 3 st wrap, [p1, k1tbl] 1 (2) times; repeat from * to end of rnd.
Rnd 4: *P1, [k1tbl, p1] 0 (1) time, 3 st wrap, p1, 3 st wrap, [p1, k1tbl] four times, p1, 3 st wrap, p1, 3 st wrap, [p1, k1tbl] 0 (1) time; repeat from * to end of rnd.
Rnd 6: *[P1, k1tbl] 1 (2) times p1, 3 st wrap, [p1, k1tbl] six times, p1, 3 st wrap, [p1, k1tbl] 1 (2) times; repeat from * to end of rnd.
Rnd 8: As Rnd 4.
Rnd 10: As Rnd 2.
Rnd 12: *[P1, k1tbl] 4 (5) times, p1, 3 st wrap, p1, 3 st wrap, [p1, k1tbl] 4 (5) times; repeat from * to end of rnd.
Rnd 14: *[P1, k1tbl] 5 (6) times, p1, 3 st wrap, [p1, k1tbl] 5 (6) times; repeat from * to end of rnd.
Rnd 16: As Rnd 12.

Thumb gusset
Rnd 1: M2pkp, pm, work remaining sts in patt as established.
Rnd 2: P1, k1tbl, p1, sm, work remaining sts in patt as established.

To keep the continuity of the p1, k1tbl rib for the thumb increases, work one of the following for each increase.
At the beginning of the gusset:
If your first two sts are purls, work a M1pk into the first st.
If your first two sts are a purl and a k1tbl, work a M1pp into the first st.
At the end of the gusset:
If your last two sts are a k1tbl, and a purl, work a M1pp into the last st.
If your last two sts are purls, work a M1kp into the last st.

Rnd 3: Work increase into first st, work to last st before marker keeping continuity of p1, k1tbl rib, work in pattern to end of rnd.
Rnd 4: Work sts as they appear.
Continue increasing every odd rnd until there are 19 (23) sts before the marker, keeping continuity of p1, k1tbl rib.

Try on the mitten. If the gusset reaches your thumb divide, continue to next rnd, if not, work rnds in pattern without increasing until it does.
Similarly, if the gusset needs to be wider, add more increases until it's the desired width.

Thumb divide

Slip sts before marker onto waste yarn.

Using backwards loop method, cast on 1 st in MC, work in pattern to end of rnd.

Continue working in pattern as established until 3 full repeats of *pattern name stitch* have been completed, or mitt is 1.5 inches / 3.75 cm shorter than desired total length.

Work p1, k1tbl corrugated rib for 1.5 inches / 3.75 cm. Bind off in pattern.

Thumb

Place sts from waste yarn back onto needles, and arrange them for small circumference knitting.

Rnd 1: With MC, pick up and purl 3 sts in the p1 st at the thumb divide.

Rnd 2: Work p1, k1tbl corrugated rib for 1.5 inches / 3.75 cm, or to desired height. Bind off in pattern.

Weave in ends.

Wet block to measurements (blocking instructions page 13).

Chart (read bottom to top, rows 1–16):

16	Я • Я • Я • Я • Я • ←3→ • ←3→ • Я • Я • Я • Я • Я •
15	Я • Я • Я • Я • Я • Я • Я • Я • Я • Я • Я • Я • Я •
14	Я • Я • Я • Я • Я • Я • ←3→ • Я • Я • Я • Я • Я • Я •
13	Я • Я • Я • Я • Я • Я • Я • Я • Я • Я • Я • Я • Я •
12	Я • Я • Я • Я • Я • ←3→ • ←3→ • Я • Я • Я • Я • Я •
11	Я • Я • Я • Я • Я • Я • Я • Я • Я • Я • Я • Я • Я •
10	Я • Я • ←3→ • Я • Я • ←3→ • Я • Я • ←3→ • Я • Я • Я •
9	Я • Я • Я • Я • Я • Я • Я • Я • Я • Я • Я • Я • Я •
8	Я • ←3→ • ←3→ • Я • Я • Я • Я • ←3→ • ←3→ • Я • Я •
7	Я • Я • Я • Я • Я • Я • Я • Я • Я • Я • Я • Я • Я •
6	Я • Я • ←3→ • Я • Я • Я • Я • Я • ←3→ • Я • Я • Я •
5	Я • Я • Я • Я • Я • Я • Я • Я • Я • Я • Я • Я • Я •
4	Я • ←3→ • ←3→ • Я • Я • Я • ←3→ • ←3→ • Я • Я •
3	Я • Я • Я • Я • Я • Я • Я • Я • Я • Я • Я • Я • Я •
2	Я • Я • ←3→ • Я • Я • ←3→ • Я • Я • ←3→ • Я • Я • Я •
1	Я • Я • Я • Я • Я • Я • Я • Я • Я • Я • Я • Я • Я •

Column numbering (Medium): 24 23 22 21 20 19 18 17 16 15 14 13 12 11 10 9 8 7 6 5 4 3 2 1

Column numbering (Large): 28 27 26 25 24 23 22 21 20 19 18 17 16 15 14 13 12 11 10 9 8 7 6 5 4 3 2 1

Legend:

Я	Knit
•	Purl
←3→	3st wrap

| Medium - work within these lines

| Large - work within these lines

WHITE LIGHT/WHITE HEAT

An ombre ball of yarn paired with a solid, standout cable color makes the stitches pop even more. I recommend Freia Fibers' ombre yarns because they have long, smooth color transitions compared to using gradient kits or self-striping style yarns.

REQUIRED SKILLS

Working Color Cables from chart or written instructions
Wrap stitch

SIZE

One size

FINISHED MEASUREMENTS

6.25 inches / 15.75 cm wide x 80 inches / 203.25 cm long

Note: I loved the wavy texture of this scarf so much that I decided not to block it. If you do block, the measurements will grow slightly.

MATERIALS

Freia Fine Handpaints Sport (100% wool; 145 yds / 133 m per 50 g / 1.76 oz ball)
MC color: Ecru: 2 balls
Freia Fine Handpaints Sport (100% wool; 217 yds / 198 m per 75 g / 2.65 oz ball
CC color: Fuchsia: 2 balls
US#6 / 4 mm needles or size needed to obtain gauge
Cable needle
Large-eyed, blunt needle

GAUGE

30 sts x 26 rows = 4 inches in stitch pattern

PATTERN NOTES

I used two skeins of gradient yarn for this scarf, and worked from the inside out on one skein and from the outside in on the other to ensure the fuchsia colors were at the beginning and end of the scarf.

ABBREVIATIONS

cn — cable needle
k — knit
p — purl
st(s) stitch(es)
wyib — with yarn in back
wyif — with yarn in front

TECHNIQUES

Note: see pages 23— for cable technique instructions
2/1 LpC — slip 2 sts to cn, hold in front, with MC p1, with CC k2 from cn
2/1 RpC — slip 1 st to cn, hold in back, with CC k2, with MC p1 from cn
2/2 LpC — slip 2 sts to cn, hold in front, with MC p2, with CC k2 from cn
2/2 RpC — slip 2 sts to cn, hold in back, with CC k2, with MC p2 from cn
4 st wrap — [wyib, slip 4 sts to RH needle, wyif, slip 4 sts back to LH needle] three times, CC k4.

PATTERN

Using long-tail method, and with MC, cast on 48 sts.
Row 1: MC k3, p3 [CC k4, MC p4] 4 times, CC k4, MC p3, k3.
Row 2: MC k6, [CC p4, MC k4] 4 times, CC p4, MC k6.
Row 3: MC k3, p3, [4 st wrap, MC p4] 4 times, 4 st wrap, MC p3, k3.
Row 4 (and all even rows): Maintaining 3 st garter band at beginning and end, work sts as they appear.
Row 5: MC k3, p1, [2/2 RpC, 2/2 LpC, MC p2, CC k4, MC p2] twice, 2/2 RpC, 2/2 LpC, MC p1, k3.
Row 7: MC k3, [2/1 RpC, MC p4, 2/1 LpC, MC p1, 4 st wrap, MC p1] twice, 2/1 RpC, MC p4, 2/1 LpC, MC k3.
Row 9: MC k3, [2/1 LpC, MC p4, 2/1 RpC, p1, CC k4, MC p1] twice, 2/1 LpC, CC p4, 2/1 RpC, MC k3.
Row 11: MC k3, p1, [2/2 LpC, 2/2 RpC, MC p2, 4 st wrap, MC p2] twice, 2/2 LpC, 2/2 RpC, MC p1, k3.
Row 13: MC k3, p3, [4 st wrap, MC p2, 2/2 RpC, 2/2 LpC, MC p2] twice, 4 st wrap, MC p3, k3.
Row 15: MC k3, p3, [CC k4, MC p1, 2/1 RpC, MC p4, 2/1 LpC, MC p1] twice, CC k4, MC p3, k3.
Row 17: MC k3, p3, [4 st wrap, MC p1, 2/1 LpC, MC p4, 2/1 RpC, MC p1] twice, 4 st wrap, MC p3, k3.

Row 19: MC k3, p3, [CC k4, MC p2, 2/2 LpC, 2/2 RpC, MC p2] twice, CC k4, MC p3, k3.

Work repeats of Rows 3 — 20 until scarf is desired length.
Break CC.
With MC only, bind off in pattern.

Weave in ends.

Wet block if you prefer, however, the luscious texture of this scarf begs to not be blocked!

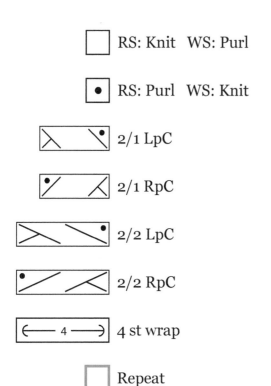

RS: Knit WS: Purl

RS: Purl WS: Knit

2/1 LpC

2/1 RpC

2/2 LpC

2/2 RpC

4 st wrap

Repeat

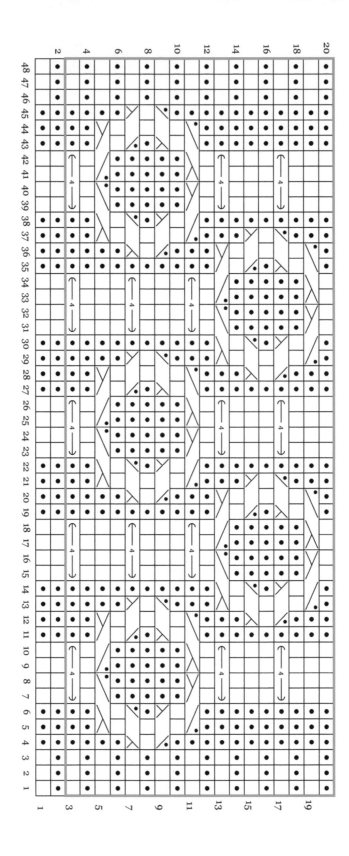

FASCINATION

If you have never tried an I-cord cast on or bind off, then you are in for a real treat. This technique creates a superbly polished edge, which also adds structure and reduces the likelihood of over-stretching. All of which are ideal characteristics in a cowl you'll want to wear through multiple seasons. This cozy cowl features an easy-to-knit cable design with simple right and left crosses, plus it highlights the use of a mini-gradient kit. So the next time you drool over those stunning and inviting mini-skein sets, you'll have even more reason to take one — or two — home.

REQUIRED SKILLS

I-cord cast on and bind off
Backwards loop cast on
Working in the round
Working basic cables from chart or written directions
Color Cable techniques

SIZE

One size

FINISHED MEASUREMENTS

Before blocking: 25 inches / 63.5 cm circumference x 10.5 inches / 26.75 cm height
After blocking: 27 inches / 66.5 cm circumference x 12 inches / 30.5 cm height

MATERIALS

Pigeonroof Studios High Twist Sock (100% merino; 400 yds / 366 m per skein)
MC color: Celeste: 1 skein
Pigeonroof Studios High Twist Sock Minis (100% merino; 240 yds / 219 m per six mini skein set): 1 set
CC color: Fresas
US#3 / 3.25 mm needles, configured for circular knitting, or size needed to

obtain gauge
US#3 / 3.25 mm double-pointed needles
Cable needle
Large-eyed, blunt needle

GAUGE

26 sts and 26 rnds = 4 inches / 10 cm in color cable pattern, after blocking.

PATTERN NOTES

When working with two colors of yarn, wrap one yarn around the other every time they meet for the first time on each row. This locks the yarns together and avoids holes.

Carry your floats loosely across the WS of your work. On all rounds, work knit stitches in CC, and purl stitches in MC. If working from the chart, it's helpful to color all the knit stitches in the color of your CC yarn, and the purl stitches the color of your MC yarn.

ABBREVIATIONS

CC — contrasting color
cn — cable needle
dpns — double-pointed needles
k — knit
MC — main color
p — purl
pm — place marker
rnd(s) — round(s)
st(s) — stitch(es)
WS — wrong side

TECHNIQUES

Note: see pages 23— for cable technique instructions
I-cord cast on <link> https://newstitchaday.com/how-to-knit-the-i-cord-cast-on/
I-cord bind off <link> https://newstitchaday.com/how-to-knit-the-i-cord-bind-off/
2/1 LpC — slip 2 sts to cn, hold in front, with MC p1, with CC k2 from cn
2/1 RpC — slip 1 st to cn, hold in back, with CC k2, with MC p1 from cn
2/2 LC — slip 2 sts to cn, hold in front, with CC k2, with CC k2 from cn
2/2 RC — slip 2 sts to cn, hold in back, with CC k2, with CC k2 from cn

FASCiNATioN STiTCH PATTERN

Rnd 1: P2, 2/1 LpC, p4, 2/2 RC, p2, 2/2 RC, p4, 2/1 RpC, p2.
Rnd 2 (and all even rnds): Work sts as they appear.
Rnd 3: P3, 2/1 LpC, p2, 2/1 RpC, 2/1 LpC, 2/1 RpC, 2/1 LpC, p2, 2/1 RpC, p3.
Rnd 5: P4, 2/1 LpC, 2/1 RpC, p2, 2/2 LC, p2, 2/1 LpC, 2/1 RpC, p4.
Rnd 7: P5, 2/2 LC, p3, k4, p3, 2/2 RC, p5.
Rnd 9: P4, 2/1 RpC, 2/1 LpC, p2, 2/2 LC, p2, 2/1 RpC, 2/1 LpC, p4.
Rnd 11: P3, 2/1 RpC, p2, 2/1 LpC, 2/1 RpC, 2/1 LpC, 2/1 RpC, p2, 2/1 LpC, p3.
Rnd 13: P2, 2/1 RpC, p4, 2/2 LC, p2, 2/2 LC, p4, 2/1 LpC, p2.
Rnd 15: P1, 2/1 RpC, p4, 2/1 RpC, 2/1 LpC, 2/1 RpC, 2/1 LpC, p4, 2/1 LpC, p1.
Rnd 17: P1, k2, p4, 2/1 RpC, p2, 2/2 LC, p2, 2/1 LpC, p4, k2, p1.
Rnd 19: P1, 2/1 LpC, p2, 2/1 RpC, p3, k4, p3, 2/1 LpC, p2, 2/1 RpC, p1.
Rnd 21: P2, 2/1 LpC, 2/1 RpC, p4, 2/2 LC, p4, 2/1 LpC 2/1 RpC, p2.
Rnd 23: P3, 2/2 RC, p5, k4, p5, 2/2 RC, p3.
Rnd 25: P2, 2/1 RpC, 2/1 LpC, p4, 2/2 LC, p4, 2/1 RpC, 2/1 LpC, p2.
Rnd 27: P1, 2/1 RpC, p2, 2/1 LpC, p3, k4, p3, 2/1 RpC, p2, 2/1 LpC, p1.
Rnd 29: P1, k2, p4, 2/1 LpC, p2, 2/2 LC, p2, 2/1 RpC, p4, k2, p1.
Rnd 31: P1, 2/1 LpC, p4, 2/1 LpC, 2/1 RpC, 2/1 LpC, 2/1 RpC, p4, 2/1 RpC, p1.

PATTERN

I-cord cast on
Using two dpns, and MC, cast on 4 sts, and work I-cord as follows:
Rnd 1: Slide sts to beginning of cast on needle, carry yarn across back of sts, and knit.
Rnds 2 — 196: Repeat Rnd 1.

Working with your circular needle, bind off 3 sts, pick up and knit 196 sts, which is 1 st for each rnd worked along the I-cord. Pm, join to work in the round.

Foundation Rnd: [P3, k2, p4, k4, p2, k4, p4, k2, p3] seven times.
Rnd 1: Using MC for purls, and CC for knits, work Rnd 1 of Fascination chart or written stitch directions above. Work 7 total repeats across the rnd.

Continue, working two full repeats of Rnds 1 — 32, then Rnd 1 once.

Break CC yarn.

Rnd 67: With MC only, [p2, k2, p5, k4, p2, k4, p5, k2, p2] seven times.

I-cord bind off
With one dpn, using backwards loop cast on, cast on 4 sts.
Rnd 1: Slide 4 sts to beginning of dpn, carry yarn across back of sts, k3, ssk, incorporating one st from cowl.
Repeat Rnd 1 across cowl until 4 sts remain.
Bind off.

Weave in all ends.

Wet block to measurements (blocking instructions page 13).

☐ Knit

⊡ Purl

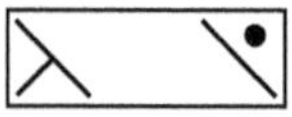

2/1 LpC

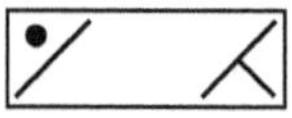

2/1 RpC

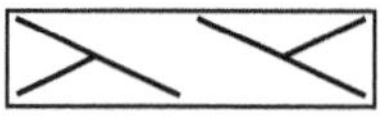

2/2 LC

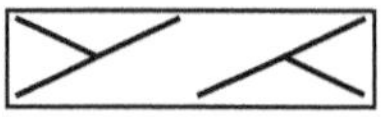

2/2 RC

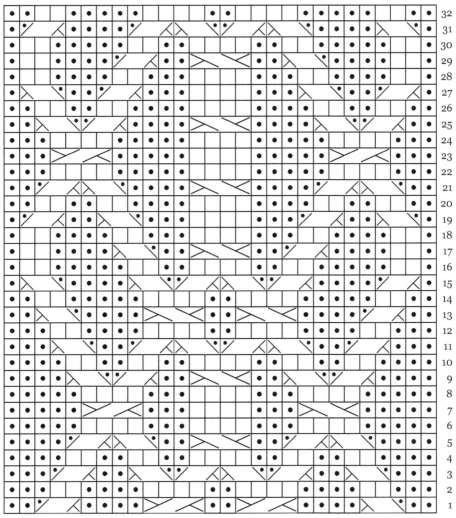

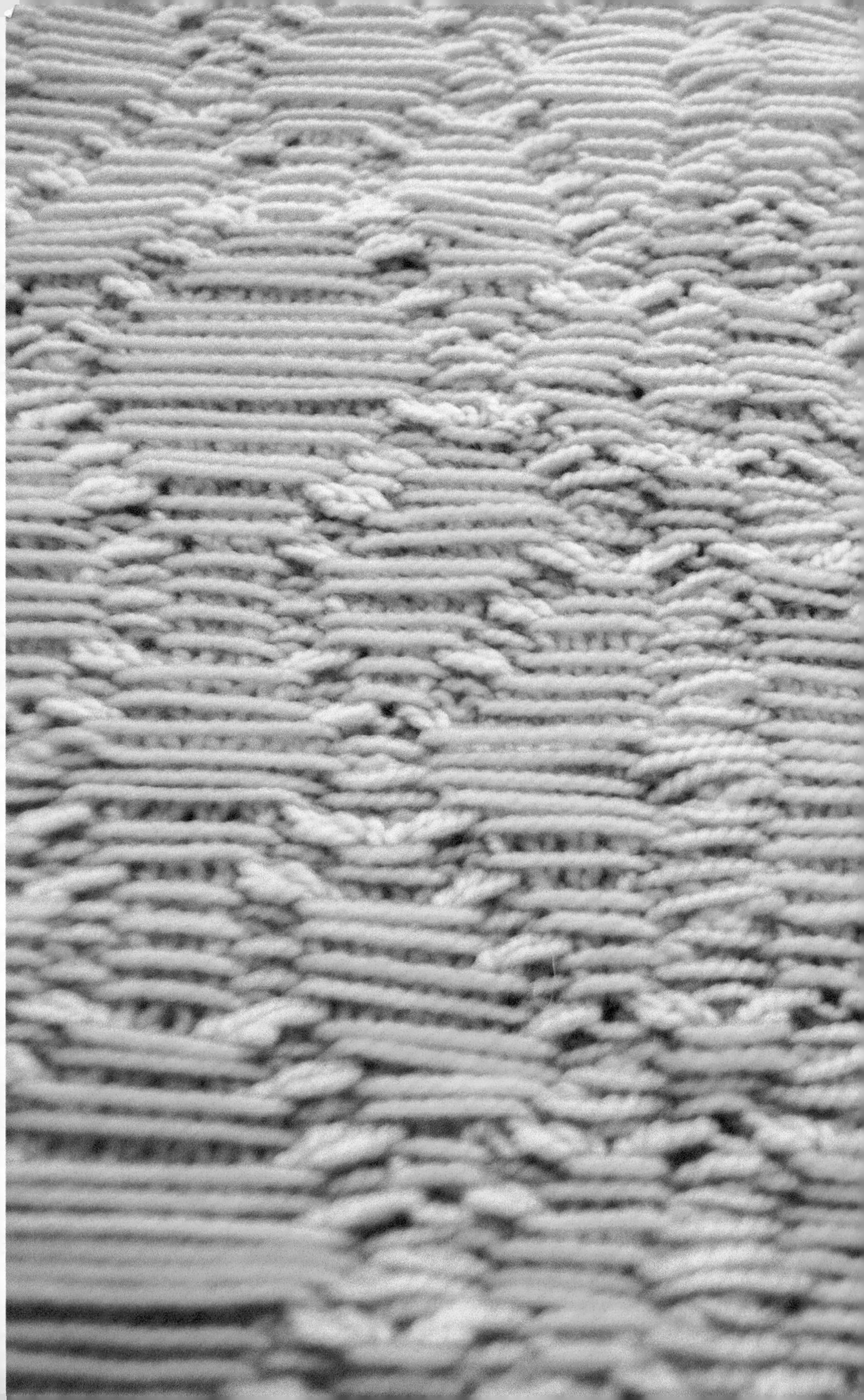

UP THE HILL BACKWARDS

Much like the Fascination cowl pattern (page 59), this scarf also features easy-to-knit cables with simple right and left crosses, they just occur a bit more frequently. When knit in leafy shades of green, as with this mini skein set from Pigeonroof Studios, the cables take on a Celtic flair that impress everyone at knit night and beyond!

REQUIRED SKILLS

Working basic cables from chart or written directions
Color Cable techniques

SIZE

One size

FINISHED MEASUREMENTS

Before blocking: 5.75 inches / 14.5 cm wide x 50 inches / 127 cm long
After blocking: 5.5 inches / 14.5 cm wide x 56 inches / 142.25 cm long

MATERIALS

Pigeonroof Studios High Twist Sock (100% merino; 400 yds / 366 m per skein)
MC color: Charcoal: 1 skein
Pigeonroof Studios High Twist Sock Minis (100% merino; 240 yds / 219 m per six mini skein set),
CC color: Celery: 1 set
US#2 / 3 mm needles, or size needed to obtain gauge
Cable needle
Large-eyed, blunt needle

GAUGE

36 sts and 32 rows = 4 inches / 10 cm in color cable pattern, unblocked
34 sts and 28 rnds in color cable pattern, blocked.

PATTERN NOTES

When working with two colors of yarn, wrap one yarn around the other every time they meet for the first time on each row. This locks the yarns together and avoids holes.

Carry your floats loosely across the WS of your work. On RS rows, work all knit sts in CC, and all purl sts in MC. On WS rows, work all knit sts in MC, and all purl sts in CC.

If working from the chart, it's helpful to color all the knit sts in the color of your CC yarn, and your purl sts the color of your MC yarn.

ABBREVIATIONS

CC — contrasting color
cn — cable needle
k — knit
MC — main color
p — purl
RS — right side
st(s) — stitch(es)
WS — wrong side

TECHNIQUES

Note: see pages 23— for cable technique instructions
2/1 LpC — slip 2 sts to cn, hold in front, with MC p1, with CC k2 from cn
2/1 RpC — slip 1 st to cn, hold in back, with CC k2, with MC p1 from cn
2/2 LC — slip 2 sts to cn, hold in front, with CC k2, with CC k2 from cn
2/2 RC — slip 2 sts to cn, hold in back, with CC k2, with CC k2 from cn

PATTERN

Using your favorite stretchy method, cast on 52 sts in MC.
Foundation Row 1(RS): [P2, k2] twice, [p2, k4, p2, k2, p2, k2] three times, p2.
Foundation Row 2(WS): [K2, p2] twice, [k2, p4, k2, p2, k2, p2] three times, k2.
Work repeats of Foundation Rows 1 and 2 until scarf measures 4 inches / 10 cm long.

Working from either the written instructions below, or from the chart, work repeats of Rows 1 — 36, changing CC colors as necessary.

Row 1: P2, k2, [p2, k2, p2, 2/2 RC, p2, k2] three times, p2, k2, p2.

Row 2 (and all even rows): Work sts as they appear.

Row 3: P2, k2, [p2, 2/1 LpC, 2/1 RpC, 2/1 LpC, 2/1 RpC,] three times, p2, k2 p2.

Row 5: P2, k2, [p3, 2/2 RC, p2, 2/2 LC, p1] three times, p2, k2, p2.

Row 7: P2, k2, [p2, 2/1 RpC, 2/1 LpC, 2/1 RpC, 2/1 LpC] three times, p2, k2 p2.

Row 9: P2, k2, [p2, k2, p2, 2/2 RC, p2, k2] three times, p2, k2, p2.

Row 11: P2, k2, [p2, k2, p1, 2/1 RpC, 2/1 LpC, p1, k2] three times, p2, k2, p2.

Row 13: P2, k2, [p2, k2, 2/1 RpC, p2, 2/1 LpC, k2] three times, p2, k2, p2.

Row 15: P2, k2, [p2, 2/2 RC, p4, 2/2 LC] three times, p2, k2, p2.

Row 17: P2, k2, [p2, k4, p4, k4] three times, p2, k2, p2.

Row 19: P2, k2, [p2, 2/2 RC, p4, 2/2 LC] three times, p2, k2, p2.

Row 21: P2, k2, [p2, k2, 2/1 LpC, p2, 2/1 RpC, k2] three times, p2, k2, p2.

Row 23: P2, k2, [p2, k2, p1, 2/1 LpC, 2/1 RpC, p1, k2] three times, p2, k2, p2.

Row 25: P2, k2, [p2, k2, p2, 2/2 LC, p2, k2] three times, p2, k2, p2.

Row 27: P2, k2, [p2, 2/1 LpC, 2/1 RpC, 2/1 LpC, 2/1 RpC] three times, p2, k2, p2.

Row 29: P2, k2, [p3, 2/2 LC, p2, 2/2 RC, p1] three times, p2, k2, p2.

Row 31: P2, k2, [p2, 2/1 RpC, 2/1 LpC, 2/1 RpC, 2/1 LpC] three times, p2, k2 p2.

Row 33: P2, k2, [p2, k2, p2, 2/2 RC, p2, k2] three times, p2, k2, p2.

Row 35: P2, k2, [p2, k4, p4, k4] three times, p2, k2, p2.

Continue as set until the scarf is 4 inches / 10 cm shorter than desired length, or the last color section is 4 inches / 10 cm shorter than the first color section, ending after Row 10, Row 26, or Row 34.

Work Foundation Rows 1 and 2 for 4 inches / 10 cm. Break CC yarn. Bind off in pattern using MC only.

Weave in all ends.

Wet block to measurements (blocking instructions page 13).

☐ RS: Knit WS: Purl

▣ RS:Purl WS: Knit

2/1 LpC

2/1 RpC

2/2 LC

2/2 RC

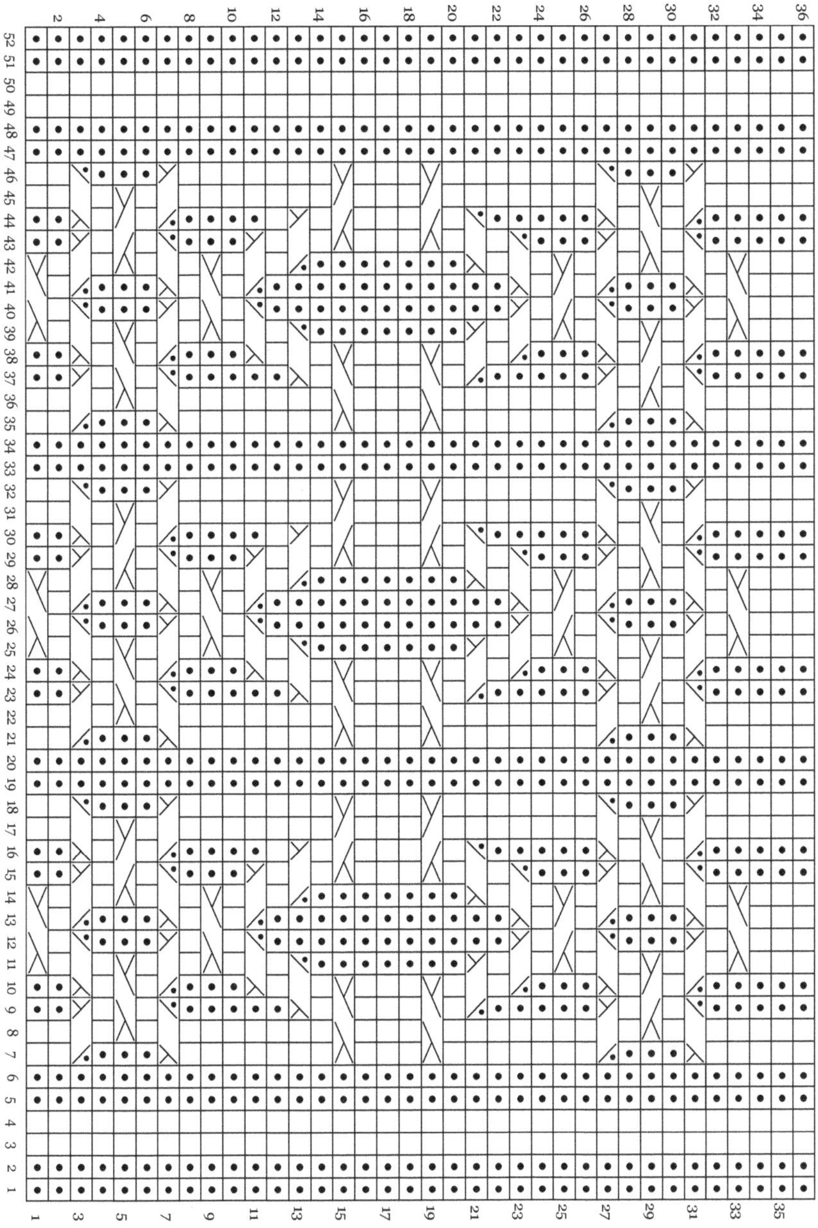

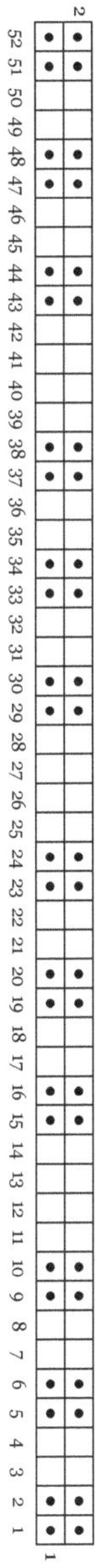

Foundation Rows

OH! YOU PRETTY THINGS

The cool aquatic tones in this Neighborhood Fiber Company gradient set serve as a suitable backdrop for a rich purple semi-solid cable on the edge of this asymmetric shawl. A simple rolled edge along the two shorter sides gives the illusion of an i-cord bind-off without the hassle of making one.

REQUIRED SKILLS

I-cord bind off
Working cables from chart or written directions
Color cable techniques

SIZE

One size

FINISHED MEASUREMENTS

67 inches / 170.25 cm wingspan x 22 inches / 55.75 cm tall after blocking

MATERIALS

Neighborhood Fiber Co Rustic Fingering (100% merino; 1250 yds / 1143 m per 300 g 5 skein set)
MC color: Shades of Jade: 1 set
Neighborhood Fiber Co Rustic Fingering (100% merino; 475 yds / 434 m per 114 / 4.02 oz skein)
CC color: Palisades : 1 set
US#4 / 3.5 mm needles, configured for circular knitting, or size needed to obtain gauge
US#4 / 3.5 mm double-pointed needles
2 stitch markers
Cable needle
Large-eyed, blunt needle

GAUGE

23 sts and 44 rows = 4 inches / 10 cm in garter stitch

PATTERN NOTES

When working with two colors of yarn, wrap one yarn around the other every time they meet for the first time on each row. This locks the yarns together and avoids holes. Carry your floats loosely across the WS of your work.

On RS rows, work knit stitches in CC, and purl stitches in MC.

On WS rows, work knit stitches in MC and purl stitches in CC.

If working from the chart, it's helpful to color all the knit stitches in the color of your CC yarn, and the purl stitches the color of your MC yarn.

ABBREVIATIONS

CC — contrasting color
cn — cable needle
dpn — double-pointed needle
k — knit
MC — main color
p — purl
pm — place marker
RS — right side
sm — slip marker
st(s) — stitch(es)
WS — wrong side
yo — yarn over

TECHNIQUES

Note: see pages 23— for cable technique instructions
m1 — make 1 by picking up bar between 2 sts, and knitting it
m1p — make 1 by picking up the bar between 2 sts, and purling it
1/1 LC — slip 1 st to cn, hold in front, with CC k1, with CC k1 from cn
1/1 LpC — slip 1 st to cn, hold in front, with MC p1, with CC k1 from cn
1/1 RC — slip 1 st to cn, hold in back, with CC k1, with CC k1 from cn
1/1 RpC — slip 1 st to cn, hold in back, with CC k1, with MC p1 from cn
2/1 LpC — slip 2 sts to cn, hold in front, with MC p1, with CC k2 from cn
2/1 RpC — slip 1 st to cn, hold in back, with CC k2, with MC p1 from cn
2/2 RC — slip 2 sts to cn, hold in back, with CC k2, with CC k2 from cn

OH! You PRETTY ThiNGS STitCH PATTERN

Row 1: P2, 1/1 LpC, 1/1 RpC, p5, 2/2 RC, p5, 1/1 LpC, 1/1 RpC, p2.

Row 2 (and all even rows): Work sts as they appear.

Row 3: P3, 1/1 LC, p5, 2/1 RpC, 2/1 LpC, p5, 1/1 RC, p3.

Row 5: P2, 1/1 RpC, 1/1 LpC, p3, 2/1 RpC, p2, 2/1 LpC, p3, 1/1 RpC, 1/1 LpC, p2.

Row 7: [P2, k1] twice, p2, 2/1 RpC, k4, 2/1 LpC, p2, [k1, p2] twice.

Row 9: P2, 1/1 LpC, 1/1 RpC, p1, 2/1 RpC, p1, 2/2 RC, p1, 2/1 LpC, p1, 1/1 LpC, 1/1 RpC, p2.

Row 11: P3, 1/1 LC, [p1, 2/1 RpC] twice, [2/1 LpC, p1] twice, 1/1 RC, p3.

Row 13: P5, 2/1 RpC, p1, 2/1 RpC, p2, 2/1 LpC, p1, 2/1 LpC, p5.

Row 15: P4, 2/1 RpC, p1, 2/1 RpC, p4, 2/1 LpC, p1, 2/1 LpC, p4.

Row 17: P3, 2/1 RpC, p2, 2/1 LpC, p4, 2/1 RpC, p2, 2/1 LpC, p3.

Row 19: P2, 1/1 RpC 1/1 LpC, p3, 2/1 LpC, p2, 2/1 RpC p3, 1/1 RpC, 1/1/ LpC, p2.

Row 21: [P2, k1] twice, p4, 2/1 LpC, 2/1 RpC, p4, [k1, p2] twice.

PATTERN

Row 1 (RS): With MC k3, work Row 1 of chart or written instructions below across next 26 sts, drop CC, pm, with MC only yo, pm, m1p, k3. 2 sts increased.

Row 2 (WS): With MC p3, sm, m1, knit to next marker, sm, work Row 2 of chart or written instructions below across next 26 sts, p3. 1 st increased.

Row 3: With MC k3, work next row of cable pattern across next 26 sts, sm, with MC only yo, knit to next m, m1p, sm, k3. 2 sts increased.

Row 4: With MC p3, sm, m1, knit to next marker, sm, work next row of cable pattern across next 26 sts, p3. 1 st increased.

Repeat Rows 3 and 4 until you are out of MC yarn, or shawl is desired width, ending after a WS row.

Button loop

Break MC, and working with CC only:

Using dpns, knit first 3 sts.

Row 1:Slide sts to beginning of needle, carry yarn across back of work to beginning of sts.

Repeat Row 1, creating a button loop 3 inches / 7.5 cm long.

I-cord bind off

Rnd 1: Slide 3 sts to beginning of dpn, carry yarn across back of sts, k2, ssk, incorporating one st from cowl.

Repeat Rnd 1 across cowl until 3 sts remain.

Bind off.

Weave in all ends.

Wet block to measurements (blocking instructions page 13).

☐ RS: Knit WS: Purl

• RS: Purl WS: Knit

1/1 LC

1/1 LpC

1/1 RC

1/1 RpC

2/1 LpC

2/1 RpC

2/2 RC

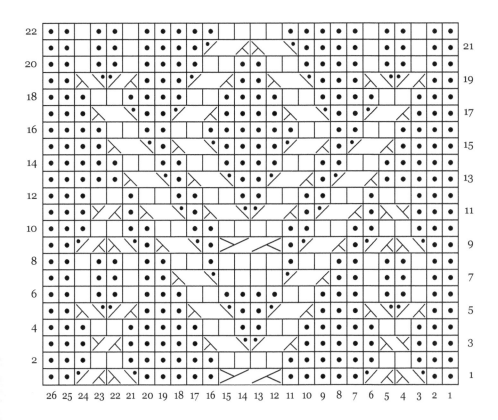

MOONAGE DAYDREAM

The next time you are out yarn shopping, pick out two complimentary gradient skeins (in fingering weight) and set them aside for this project. With this hat pattern, you can knit two hats with a completely different look from the same skeins. Hats are always a great way to try new skills and new yarn without a huge investment in time and money. The cables in this project are gorgeous and very effective in how they twist and creep toward the crown. Give the German Twisted cast on a try for a stretchy beginning, perfect for ribbing on a hat. This hat was originally published in Knit Edge magazine 10 as "Conundrum."

REQUIRED SKILLS

Decreases
German Twisted cast on (or other stretchy cast on)
Knitting in the round
Two Color cable techniques
Working cables from charted instructions

SIZES

S (M, L)

FINISHED MEASUREMENTS

(to be worn with about an inch of negative ease)
Circumference 15 (18, 22) inches / 38 (45.75, 55.75) cm
To fit 14 — 16 (17 — 19, 20 — 23) inches / 35.5 — 40.75 (43.25 — 48.25, 50.75 — 58.5) cm

MATERIALS

KnitCircus Yarns Greatest of Ease Superfine (80% Superwash Merino, 20% Nylon; 400 yds per 100 g skein; MC: April Skies, CC: Fashion Week; 1 skein of each

Note: there's enough yarn in these skeins to make 3 hats!

2 sets 16 inch US#3 / 3.25 mm circular needles, or needles needed to achieve gauge
Cable needle (optional)
Large-eyed, blunt needle

GAUGE

26 sts and 32 rnds in rib patt = 4 inches / 10 cm
30 sts and 32 rnds in color cable pattern = 4 inches / 10 cm

ABBREVIATIONS

CC — contrasting color
cn — cable needle
dec — decrease
k — knit
k2tog — knit 2 sts together
kfb — knit through the front and back loop of the same stitch
MC — main color
p — purl
p2tog — purl 2 sts together
RS — right side
ssk — slip slip knit
st(s) — stitch(es)
WS — wrong side

TECHNIQUES

Note: see pages 23— for cable technique instructions

- German twisted cast on: http://bit.ly/germantwistedCO
- 2/1 LC — slip 2 sts to cn, hold in front, CC k1, CC k2 from cn
- 2/1 LpC — slip 2 sts to cn, hold in front, MC p1, CC k2 from cn
- 2/1 RC — slip 1 st to cn, hold in back CC k1, CC k2 from cn
- 2/1 RpC — slip 1 st to cn, hold in back, CC k2, MC p1 from cn
- 2/2 LC — slip 2 sts to cn, hold in front, CC k2, CC k2 from cn
- 2/2 LpC — slip 2 st to cn, hold in front, MC p2, CC k2 from cn
- 2/2 RC — slip 2 sts to cn, hold in back, CC k2, CC k2 from cn
- 2/2 RpC — slip 2 sts to cn, hold in back, CC k2, MC p2 from cn
- 2/2 LpC dec — slip 2 sts to cn, hold in front, MC p2tog, CC k2 from cn
- 2/2 RpC dec — slip 2 sts to cn, hold in back, CC k2, MC p2tog from cn

PATTERN

With MC, using German Twisted, or your favorite stretchy method, cast on 80 (100, 120) sts. Being careful not to twist, join to work in the round, arranging the sts evenly over two needles.

Rib
Rnd 1: *P1, k2, p4, k2 [p2, k2] twice, p3; repeat from * around.
Work repeats of rib round for 2 (2.5, 3) inches / 5 (6.25, 7.75) cm.
Increase rnd: *P1, [kfb] twice, p4, [kfb] twice, [p2, kfb, kfb] twice, p3; repeat from * around. 112, (140, 168) sts.

Working from the chart, work 4 (5, 6) repeats of the chart around from Rnds 1 — 54, using MC for all knit sts and CC for all purl sts.

Cut yarns, thread through the live sts twice, and tighten securely.

Weave in all ends.

Wet block to measurements (blocking instructions page 13).

⬜	No stitch
⬜	Knit MC
⬜•	Purl CC
⬜╱	K2tog MC
⬜╲	Ssk CC
╲___╲	2/1 LC
╲___╲•	2/1 LpC
╱___╱	2/1 RC
•╱___╱	2/1 RpCp
╲___╲	2/2 LC
╲___╲•	2/2 LpC
╱___╱	2/2 RC
•╱___╱	2/2 RpC
╲___╲•	2/2 LpC dec
•╱___╱	2/2 RpC dec

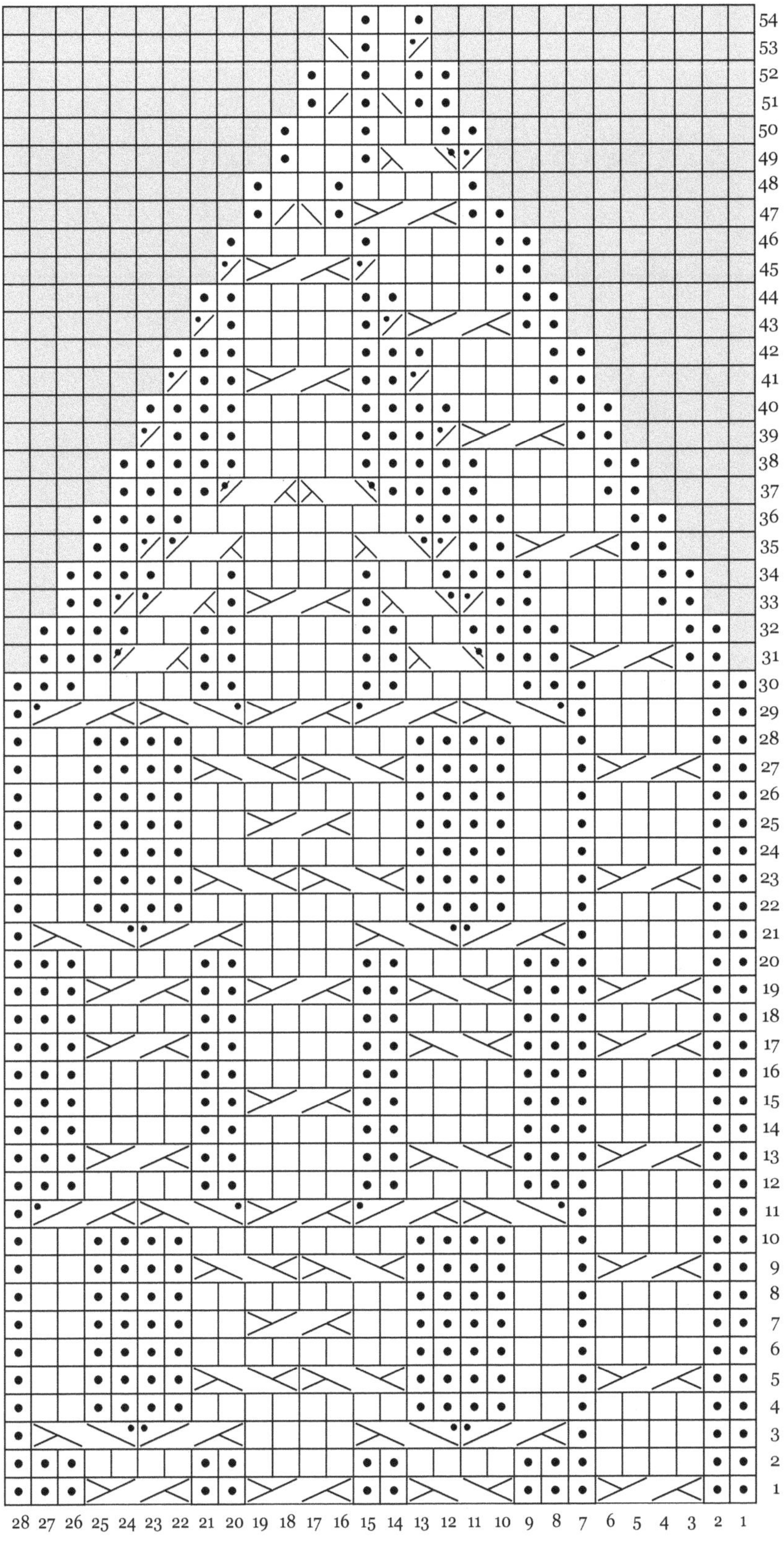
54 53 52 51 50 49 48 47 46 45 44 43 42 41 40 39 38 37 36 35 34 33 32 31 30 29 28 27 26 25 24 23 22 21 20 19 18 17 16 15 14 13 12 11 10 9 8 7 6 5 4 3 2 1
28 27 26 25 24 23 22 21 20 19 18 17 16 15 14 13 12 11 10 9 8 7 6 5 4 3 2 1

SOUL LOVE

Show your love of gradient kits with this heart cable worked into a charming scarf. Whether you choose a gradient background, mini-skein cables, two colors, or one single glorious skein, the cables pop, and the results are worth the effort.

REQUIRED SKILLS
Color Cable techniques
Working cables from written instructions or chart
3 needle bind off

SIZE
One size

FINISHED MEASUREMENTS
Before blocking: 60 inches / 152.5 cm long x 7 inches / 17.75 cm wide
After blocking: 67 inches / 170.25 cm long x 7 inches / 18.5 cm wide

MATERIALS
MC Dragonfly Fibers Dragon Sock (100% Superwash Wool; 390 yds / 357 m per 4.02 oz / 114g skein); 1 skein, MC: Cheshire Cat
CC Dragonfly Fibers Gradient Set (100% Superwash Merino; 97.5 yds per 1oz mini-skein); 1 set, CC: Winter Woods
US#3 / 3.25 mm needles, or size needed to obtain gauge
1 US#3 / 3.25 mm dpn for three needle bind off
Cable needle
Waste yarn or stitch holder
Large-eyed, blunt needle

GAUGE
30 sts and 28 rows = 4 inches / 10 cm in color cable pattern

PATTERN NOTES

Soul Love is knitted in two halves and joined with a Three Needle bind off. There is a garter stitch band on each of the short edges and a four-stitch edge flanking the cable repeats on each long side edge.

Soul Love uses almost all of the MC color, and about half of each of the mini-skeins. To make a longer scarf, be sure to get two skeins of MC, or save your minis for another Color Cable creation.

If you're working this scarf in two colors, rather than seven, at the widest point, there will be a nine-stitch float between each motif. Let the float relax against the background fabric, ensuring that you're not pulling it too tight.

Wrap each color as you get to it for the first time with the MC. If you wrap in the same direction each time, then wrap the MC in the **opposite** direction on the next stitch, then your skeins will not twist together.

Directions are given using MC or CC to denote which yarn is used for which stitch. If using the chart, color the CC sts in a contrasting color to help delineate which sts they are.

 Take note of this symbol on the chart — this is worked in MC, and purled, rather than knitted, to avoid differently colored purl bumps on the right side of the scarf.

Unless otherwise indicated, on RS rows purls are worked in MC, and knits in CC and on WS rows, knits are worked in MC and purls in CC.

ABBREVIATIONS

CC — contrasting color
cn — cable needle
k — knit
kpk — (k1, p1, k1) into next st
MC — main color
pkp — (p1, k1, p1) into next st
RS — right side
p — purl
st(s) — stitch(es)
WS — wrong side

TECHNIQUES

Note: see pages 23— for cable technique instructions
2/1 LpC — slip 2 sts to cn, hold in front, MC p1, CC k2 from cn
2/1 RpC — slip 1 st to cn, hold in back, CC k2, MC p1 from cn

2/1/2 RpC — slip next 3 sts to cn, hold in back, CC k2, MC k1 from cn, CC k2 from cn

See page 12 for helpful advice on working intarsia cables.

PATTERN

The first half of Soul Love is worked with MC and three CC colors, adding a new color for each of the three repeats across each row. The first and last four stitches of every row is worked in MC.

With MC, cast on 49 sts.
Foundation Rows 1 — 6: Knit.
Row 1: With MC k3 and p1, [MC p4, CC pkp, MC p1, CC kpk, MC p5] three times, with MC p1 and k3. 55 sts — adding a new CC color in each of the three repeats across.

Row 2: With MC k4, [k6, p2, k1, p2, k5] three times, k to end of row.
Continue to work the first and last four sts of every row in MC.
Row 3: K3 and p1, [p4, 2/1RpC, p1, 2/1 LpC, p5] three times, p1, k3.
Row 4: K4, [k5, p2, k3, p2, k4] three times, k to end of row.
Row 5: K3, p1, [p3, 2/1 RpC, p1, k1, p1, 2/1 LpC, p4] three times, p1, k3.
Row 6: K4, [k4, p2, k2, p1, p2, p2, k3] three times, k to end of row.
Row 7: K3, p1, [p2, 2/1 RpC, p1, k3, p1, 2/1 LpC, p3] three times, p1, k3.
Row 8: K4, [k3, p2, k2, p3, k2, p2, k2] three times, k to end of row.
Row 9: K3, p1, [p1, 2/1 RpC, p1, k5, p1, 2/1 LpC, p2] three times, p1, k3.
Row 10: K4, [k2, p2, k2, p5, k2, p2, p1] three times, k to end of row.
Row 11: K3, p1, [2/1 RpC, p2, k5, p2, 2/1 LpC, p1] three times, p1, k3.
Row 12: K4, [k1, p2, k3, p5, k3, p2] three times, k to end of row.
Row 13: K3, p1, [2/1 LpC, p2, 2/1/2 RpC, p2, 2/1 RpC, p1] three times, p1, k3.
Row 14: K4, [k2, p2, k2, p2, k1, p2, k2, p2, k1] three times, k to end of row.
Row 15: K3, p1, [p1, 2/1 LpC, 2/1 RpC, p1, 2/1 LpC, 2/1 RpC, p2] three times, p1, k3.
Row 16: K4, [k3, **MC p2,** CC p2, MC k3, CC p2, MC p2, k2] three times, k to end of row.
Work repeats of Rows 5 — 16 until just under half of MC is used, ending after Row 16.

Row 17: K3, p1, [p3, 2/1 RpC, p3, 2/1 LpC, p4] 3 times, p1, k3. Break CC.
Row 18: In MC only, k4, [k4, p2, k5, p2, k3] 3 times, k to end of row.

Place sts on waste yarn, or stitch holder. The second half of Soul Love is worked with MC, and second three CC colors.

After Row 18, place first set of sts onto a needle. With wrong sides together and using MC, work Three Needle bind off across all sts.

Weave in all ends, matching colors as you go.
Wet block to measurements (blocking instructions page 13).

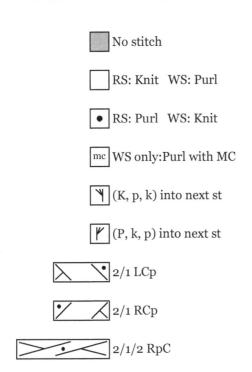

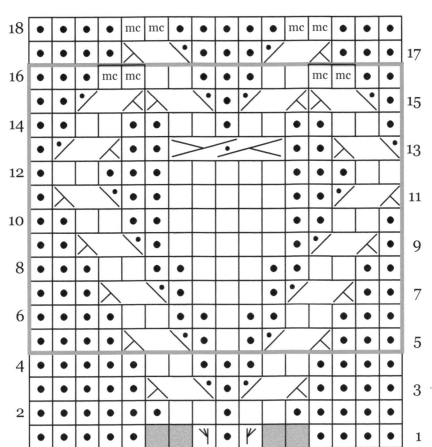

BLACKSTAR

Breaking the rules in knitting always makes me happy for some reason. When I designed this cowl, I hadn't planned on working with two different weights of yarn. I must have been distracted when I caked up the yarn, however, because it wasn't until I'd finished the swatch that I realized I'd used DK and fingering. I really liked the result though. The heavier weight, after blocking, makes the cable the absolute star!

REQUIRED SKILLS

Knitting in the round
Working cables from chart or written instructions
Color Cable techniques

SIZE

One size

FINISHED MEASUREMENTS

Before blocking: 29 inches / 73.75 cm circumference x 6.5 inches / 16.5 cm tall
After blocking: 30 inches / 76.25 cm wide x 6.5 inches / 16.5 cm tall

MATERIALS

Anzula Dreamy (75% Superwash Merino / 15% Cashmere / 10% Silk; 385 yds / 356 m per 114 g / 4.02 oz skein), 1 skein
MC color: Black: 1 skein. (approx 130 yds used)
Anzula Cricket (80% merino / 10% Cashmere / 10% Nylon; 250 yds / 228 m per 114 g / 4.02 oz skein), 1 skein
CC color: One Red Shoe: 1 skein (approx. 100 yds used)
1 set of 16 inch US#5 / 3.75 mm circular needles, or size needed to obtain gauge
Cable needle
Large-eyed, blunt needle

GAUGE

24 sts and 28 rnds = 4 inches / 10 cm in reverse stockinette st

PATTERN NOTES

This pattern has floats that are 10 stitches and 13 stitches long. To make a long float, work the stitches inside the float and spread them to gauge across the RH needle, then bring the float yarn across the back of them loosely to work the next stitch. There is no need to anchor the floats.

On Rounds 13 and 30, there are a number of stitches that are knitted in MC, rather than purled. This is done to ensure that CC purl bumps don't show in your finished cowl.

Unless otherwise stated, all purl stitches are worked in MC and all knit stitches are worked in CC.

 Take note of the symbol on the chart — this is worked in MC, and purled, rather than knitted, to avoid differently colored purl bumps on the right side of the scarf.

ABBREVIATIONS

CC — contrasting color
cn — cable needle
k — knit
k2tog — knit two sts together
MC — main color
p — purl
pw — purlwise
RH — right hand
rnd(s) — round(s)
st(s) — stitch(es)
WS — wrong side
yo — yarn over

TECHNIQUES

Note: see pages 23— for cable technique instructions
- Inc2 — (MC p1, CC k into front then back) of next st.
- Dec2 — slipw, p2tog, psso
- 2/2 LC — slip 2 sts to cn, hold in front, with CC k2, with CC k2 from cn
- 2/2 RC — slip 2 sts to cn, hold in back, with CC k2, with CC k2 from cn
- 2/2 LpC — slip 2 sts to cn, hold in front, with MC p2, with CC k2 from cn
- 2/2 RpC — slip 2 sts to cn, hold in back, with CC k2, with MC p2 from cn

- 2/3 LpC — slip 2 sts to cn, hold in front, with MC p3, with CC k2 from cn
- 2/3 RpC — slip 3 sts to cn, hold in back, with CC k2, with MC p3 from cn
- 1/2/2 LpC — slip 2 sts to cn, hold in front, with MC p1, CC k2, k2 from cn
- 2/2/1 RpC — slip 3 sts to cn, hold in back, with CC k2, (CC k2, MC p1) from cn

PATTERN

Picot edging

Using your favorite stretchy method, and MC, cast on 156 sts. Join to work in the round, being careful not to twist.

Rnds 1 — 5: Knit.

Rnd 6: *Yo, k2tog; repeat from * to end of rnd.

Rnds 7 — 11: Knit.

Rnds 12 — 14: Purl.

Working from either the written instructions below, or from the chart, work twelve repeats of the chart around from Rnds 1 — 32, using MC for all purl sts and CC for all knit sts, unless otherwise instructed.

Rnd 1: MC Purl.

Rnd 2: *MC p1, m2, p9, M2, p1; repeat from * to end of rnd. 204 sts.

Rnds 3, 4 and 5: *P2, k2, p10, k2, p1; repeat from * to end of rnd.

Rnd 6: *P2, 2/2 LC, p6, 2/2 RC, p1; repeat from * to end of rnd.

Rnd 7: *P2, k4, p6, k4, p1; repeat from * to end of rnd.

Rnd 8: *P2, k2, 2/2 LpC, p2, 2/2 RpC, k2, p1; repeat from * to end of rnd.

Rnds 9, 10 and 11: *[P2, CC k2] four times, p1; repeat from * to end of rnd.

Rnd 12: *P2, 2/2 LpC, k2, p2, k2, 2/2 RpC, p1; repeat from * to end of rnd.

Rnd 13: *P4, k2, **MC k2**, p2, MC k2, k2, p3; repeat from * to end of rnd.

Rnd 14: *P4, 2/3 LpC, 2/3 RpC, p3; repeat from * to end of rnd.

Rnd 15: P7, k4, p6; repeat from * to end of rnd.

Rnd 16: *P7, 2/2 LC, p6; repeat from * to end of rnd.

Rnd 17: *P7, k4, p6; repeat from * to end of rnd.

Rnd 18: *P4, 2/2/1 RpC, 1/2/2 LpC, p3; repeat from * to end of rnd.

Rnd 19: *P4, k4, p2, k4, p3; repeat from * to end of rnd.

Rnd 20: *P2, 2/2 RpC, k2, p2, k2, 2/2 LpC, p1; repeat from * to end of rnd.

Rnds 21, 22 and 23: *[P2, k2] four times, p1; repeat from * to end of rnd.

Rnd 24: *P2, k2, 2/2 RpC, p2, 2/2 LpC, k2, p1; repeat from * to end of rnd.

Rnd 25: *P2, k4, p6, k4, p1; repeat from * to end of rnd.

Rnd 26: *P2, 2/2 RpC, p6, 2/2 LpC, p1; repeat from * to end of rnd.

Rnd 27: *P2, k2, **MC k2**, p6, **MC k2**, k2, p1; repeat from * to end of rnd.

Rnds 28 and 29: *P2, k2, p10, k2, p1; repeat from * to end of rnd. Break CC.

Rnd 30: *With MC only, p2, k2, p10, k2, p1; repeat from * to end of rnd.

Rnd 31: *With MC only, p1, dec2, p9, dec2, p1; repeat from * to end of rnd. 156 sts.

Rnd 32: With MC only, purl.

Picot edging
Rnds 1 and 2: Purl.
Rnds 3 — 7: Knit.
Rnd 8: *Yo, k2tog; repeat from * to end of rnd.
Rnds 9 — 13: Knit.
Bind off.

Fold each picot edging at the yarn over round toward the WS. Using MC and a large-eyed blunt sewing needle, sew the stitches from the picot edging to the WS, matching stitch for stitch.

Wet block to measurements (blocking instructions page 13).

▨	No stitch
☐	Knit
mc	Knit with MC
●	Purl
⋀	Dec 2
⋁	Inc 2
	2/2 LpC
	2/2 RpC
	2/2 LC
	2/2 RC
	2/3 LpC
	2/3 RpC
	1/2/2 LpC
	2/2/1 RpC

Row numbers (right side, bottom to top): 1, 2, 3, 4, 5, 6, 7, 8, 9, 10, 11, 12, 13, 14, 15, 16, 17, 18, 19, 20, 21, 22, 23, 24, 25, 26, 27, 28, 29, 30, 31, 32

Column numbers (bottom): 17 16 15 14 13 12 11 10 9 8 7 6 5 4 3 2 1

REBEL REBEL

When a flattering shape is paired with a simple yet striking cable design, the result is a truly attractive garment. The eye-catching knot stitch in this cable breaks up the vertical stripes that run along the edge and up the slit of this skirt. The hidden elastic waistband make for a comfortable skirt to wear.

REQUIRED SKILLS

Working cables from chart or written directions
Two color cable techniques

SIZE

XS (S, M, L, 1X, 2X, 3X)

FINISHED MEASUREMENTS

After blocking:
Waist: 26 (30, 34, 38, 42, 46, 50) inches / 66 (76, 86.5, 96.5, 106.5, 117, 127) cm
Hips: 36 (40, 44, 48, 52, 56, 60) inches / 94 (101.5, 112, 122, 132, 142, 152.5) cm

To be worn with approx 1 inch / 2.5cm of negative ease
Length: 23 inches / 58.5 cm

MATERIALS

Lisa Souza Polwarth Silk DK (85% Polwarth / 15% Silk; 400 yds / 366 m per 136 g / 4.8 oz skein)
MC: All at Sea 2 (3, 3, 3, 3, 4, 4) skeins
CC: Terracotta (1 skein)
US#4 / 3.5 mm needles, configured for circular knitting, or size needed to obtain gauge
US#4 / 3.5 mm dpns
Stitch markers
Cable needle
1 inch elastic for waistband, 1 inch longer than your waist measurement.
Large-eyed, blunt needle

GAUGE

20 sts and 24 rows = 4 inches / 10 cm in stockinette, blocked

PATTERN NOTES

When working with two colors of yarn, wrap one yarn around the other every time they meet for the first time on each row. This locks the yarns together and avoids holes.

Carry your floats loosely across the WS of your work. On RS rows, work knit stitches in CC, and purl stitches in MC in the pattern section. On WS rows, work knit stitches in MC and purl stitches in CC in the pattern section.

If working from the chart, it's helpful to color all the knit stitches in the color of your CC yarn, and the purl stitches the color of your MC yarn.

ABBREVIATIONS

CC - contrasting color
cn - cable needle
k - knit
k2tog - knit 2 sts together
m1 - make 1 st by knitting into the front and back of next st
MC - main color
p - purl
pm - place marker
RS - right side
sm - slip marker
st(s) - stitch(es)
WS - wrong side

TECHNIQUES

See knot stitch tutorial on page 41.
Knot stitch — with CC only:
- slip 4 sts to cn, hold in front
- K2, bring yarn to front
- Put left 2 sts from cn onto LH needle
- Move cn to back of work
- [P2 from LH needle, slide 2 purled sts back to LH needle] twice, p2 from LH needle
- K2 from cn

Rebel Rebel stitch pattern A
Row 1: [P2, k2] twice, p3.
Row 2: K3, [p2, k2] twice.
Row 3: As Row 1.

Row 4: K3, p6, k2.
Row 5: P2, knot stitch, p3.
Row 6: K3, p2, **MC p2**, p2, k2.
Row 7: As Row 1.
Row 8: As Row 2.
Row 9: As Row 1.
Row 10: As Row 2.

Rebel Rebel stitch pattern B
Row 1:[P2, k2] twice, p2.
Row 2: K2, [p2, k2] twice.
Row 3: As Row 1.
Row 4: K3, p6, k2.
Row 5: P2, knot stitch, p2.
Row 6: K2, p2, **MC p2**, p2, k2.
Row 7: As Row 1.
Row 8: As Row 2.
Row 9: As Row 1.
Row 10: As Row 2.

PATTERN

Border
Starting at the bottom of the skirt, with MC, cast on 198 (220, 242, 264, 286, 308, 330 sts.
FoundationRow 1: *P2, k2, p2, k2, p3; repeat from * to end of row.
Foundation Row 2: *K3, p2, k2, p2, k2; repeat from * to end of row.

Row 1: Work Row 1 of Rebel Rebel stitch A across the row, using MC for the purl sts, and CC for the knit sts.
Row 2: Work Row 2 of Rebel Rebel stitch A across the row, using MC for the knit sts, and CC for the purl sts.
Row 3: Repeat Row 1.
Row 4: Repeat Row 2.
Work Rows 5 - 10, then Rows 1 - 9.
Row 20(WS): * K2tog, k1, [p2, k2] twice; repeat from * to end of row: 180 (200, 220, 240, 260, 280, 300) sts.

Skirt
Break CC, and divide the remaining CC yarn into 2 equal cakes.
Row 1: Work Row 1 of Rebel Rebel stitch B across next 10 sts, using MC, and one of the small cakes for CC. With MC, knit to last 10 sts, work Row 1 of Rebel Rebel stitch B using MC and the second of the small cakes for CC.
Row 2: Work Row 2 of Rebel Rebel stitch B across next 10 sts, using MC, and one of the small cakes for CC. With MC, purl to last 10 sts, work Row 2 of Rebel Rebel stitch B.
Continue the skirt in this manner, with the knot stitch pattern across the first and last 10 sts, and stockinette across the rest of the sts.

When skirt is 10 (10, 10, 9, 9, 8, 8) inches / 25. 5 (25.5, 25.5, 22.75, 22.75, 20.25, 20.25) cm from cast on edge, work decreases as follows:

With WS facing, work 10 sts of pattern, p28 (30, 34, 38, 40, 44, 48) sts, pm, [p26 (30, 33, 36, 40, 43, 46) sts, pm] 4 times, p28 (30, 34, 38, 40, 44, 48) sts, work last 10 sts in pattern.

Decrease Row 1: Work Rebel Rebel stitch B across first 10 sts, [k to 2 sts before next marker, k2tog, sm] 5 times, k to last 10 sts, work Rebel Rebel stitch B across last 10 sts. 175 (195, 215, 235, 255, 275. 395) sts.

Decrease Rows 2 - 4: Work in patt as set.
Repeat these 4 decrease rows a further 9 times. 130 (150, 170, 190, 220, 250, 270) sts.

Work without shaping until skirt measures 22 inches / 55.75 cm, or 1 inch less than desired length. Break CC yarn.

Waist band.
With MC only,
Rows 1, 3 and 5: Knit.
Rows 2, 4 and 6: Purl.
Row 7: Purl.
Row 8: Purl.
Rows 9 and 11: Knit.
Rows 10 and 12: Purl.
Bind off

Fold waistband at the purl row toward the WS.
With MC and a large-eyed blunt sewing needle, sew the stitches from the waistband edge to the WS, leaving a gap of 2 inches / 5 cm open to feed the elastic. Feed elastic through, sew the short ends of the elastic securely together overlapping by 1 inch / 2.5 cm. Sew the gap closed.

Weave in all ends.

Wet block to measurements (blocking instructions page 13).

RS: Knit   WS: Purl

mc WS: with MC, Purl

● RS: Purl   WS: Knit

——— k ——— Knot stitch

REBEL REBEL CHART A

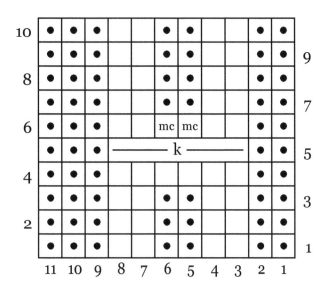

REBEL REBEL CHART B

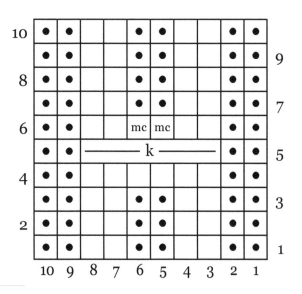

CREDiTS

This book would not be possible without the inspirational yarns from the following Indie Dyers: Sabrina, Kate and Nancye, Jaala, Amanda, Karida, Kirsta, Tina and Lisa are some of the nicest, most talented ladies you'll ever meet!

- Anzula: https://anzula.com
- Dragonfly Fibers http://www.dragonflyfibers.com
- Freia Fibers: https://freiafibers.com
- KnitCircus: https://knitcircus.com
- Lorna's Laces: http://www.lornaslaces.net
- Neighborhood Fiber Co: https://www.neighborhoodfiberco.com
- Pigeon Roof Studios: https://www.pigeonroofstudios.com
- Lisa Souza Dyeworks: http://www.lisaknit.com

Huge thanks go out to my delightful test knitters, Marie, Rebecca and Susanne. Thank you for your patience, enthusiasm, and encouragement.

The largest bucket of thanks imaginable go to Meg Roke, for tech editing my ramblings, and for being there to support me during the whole process.

All the thanks go to Shannon Okey, for all the things, always!

ABOUT ANDi

Andi Smith is a fifty-something designer, originally from England, now living in Ohio, USA. Andi is lucky enough to work as a tech editor, designer, and teacher.

Her first book, *Big Foot Knits* is available from Cooperative Press (cooperative-press.com) and her first color cable collection, Synchronicity, is available on Ravelry:

https://www.ravelry.com/patterns/sources/synchronicity/patterns

Andi can be found on

- Facebook: https://www.facebook.com/andismithdesigns
- Instagram: https://www.instagram.com/iamknitbrit
- Ravelry: https://www.ravelry.com/people/knitbrit

ABOUT CP

Cooperative Press was founded in 2007 by Shannon Okey, a voracious reader as well as writer and editor, who had been doing freelance acquisi- tions work, introducing authors with projects she believed in to editors at various publishers.

Although working with traditional publishers can be very rewarding, there are some books that fly under their radar. They're too avant–garde, or the marketing department doesn't know how to sell them, or they don't think they'll sell 50,000 copies in a year.

5,000 or 50,000. Does the book matter to that 5,000? Then it should be published.

In 2009, Cooperative Press (cooperativepress. com) changed its named to reflect the relation- ships we have developed with authors working on books. We work together to put out the best quality books we can and share in the proceeds accordingly.

Thank you for supporting independent publishers and authors.

Cooperative Press can be found on

- Facebook: http://www.facebook.com/cooperativepress
- Instagram: http://www.instagram.com/cooperativepress
- Ravelry: http://www.ravelry.com/people/cooperativepress
- Web/shop: http://cooperativepress.com

CPSIA information can be obtained
at www.ICGtesting.com
Printed in the USA
LVHW07s0430121018
593285LV00011B/18/P